D1645394

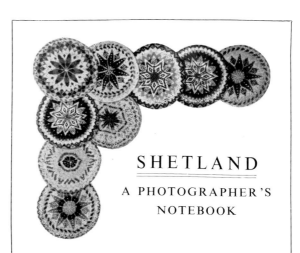

SHETLAND

A PHOTOGRAPHER'S NOTEBOOK

To
BELLE

SHETLAND

A PHOTOGRAPHER'S NOTEBOOK

By J. PETERSON A.R.P.S.

LINDSAY DRUMMOND LIMITED
2 GUILFORD PLACE LONDON WC1

FIRST PUBLISHED 1 9 4 8

R4554
Made and Printed in Great Britain
by Lund Humphries, London and Bradford

CONTENTS

ACKNOWLEDGMENT

A SUCCESSFUL photograph may tell a story, but it seldom tells anything of the story of its success. That, very often, is the result of co-operation and assistance offered by persons who do not appear in the picture, who, more often than not, would prefer not to appear, but who are willing to help when help is needed. Even such a small collection as this could not have been made without very considerable assistance from many people. And some of the results will appear as poor tributes to the efforts expended on the photographer's behalf. It is therefore with a keen awareness of this that he expresses his sense of indebtedness and appreciation of the help given him on so many occasions.

Also, to those many friends who have appeared in photographs, who have provided information, and who have given much valuable help and advice in completing the compilation, he wishes, without attempting to name them individually, to offer his grateful thanks.

5 Twageos Road
Lerwick

Arctic Tern (*Sterna macrura*, Naumann)

INTRODUCTION

I<small>N</small> bringing together these photographs, my purpose has been to present one subject—Shetland. And to offer it in a literary rather than a documentary way.

Photographers, since the days in which they could be seen, enveloped in mystery, labouring under the folds of a cumbersome focusing-cloth, have never quite outlived the artless ridicule which such technique naturally called down upon them. There was an element of stratagem, too (there still is), which fostered suspicion and led to criticism, with indictments of dodging and faking never realised outside the realms of genuine crime. And even to-day the most principled and upright of photographers have to admit that without a measure of, shall we say, manipulation, photography would be a very dull business indeed.

Perhaps the secret of all art may be successful manipulation, but what photographer, let alone a modest and discreet photographer, would venture to utter the word *art*? He may scarcely dare to suggest that manipulation is other than a questionable, almost an unpardonable, artifice. Or that it might seek vindication in the purpose for which it is being used. And, least of all, to hint that it might be used, not to misrepresent truth as a photographer comprehends it, but rather to present it in his own, if peculiar, fashion.

Be that as it may, the photographs in this collection have not been unduly manipulated; if only because manipulation requires time and skill, and the author's supply of both is limited. There are no striking new subjects, or records of rare and unusual happenings. The photographs are of commonplace things seen in ordinary circumstances—in Shetland.

The salient feature of this group of islands, in latitude sixty degrees north, longitude one degree west, can safely be said to be its cold, damp winds and the changeableness of its weather. For there is no certainty of prevailing winds; only of winds that prevail. There is but one constant, the inconstancy of the elements; one permanence, the impermanence of their moods.

And of the people? They live with their eyes on the sea and sky, perhaps not so intently as they did a little while ago, but none the less their work and comfort are still closely bound up with the rigours of an island climate in the

North Atlantic. They are prone to give the sea and sky the respect they demand, and to appreciate the occasion that lays a kindly hand upon a little space of land and water interlocked.

Island-life, fast in the grip of external forces, tends to reflect the retreat these forces dictate; it also reflects some of their serenity and stoicism. Islanders in northern latitudes become philosophers of necessity.

But of the photographs—they have been taken at odd times; not when conditions were most inviting but when opportunity allowed. Even given unlimited leisure, the photographs a photographer dreams about cannot be collected quickly, when they can be collected at all. There are too many factors outside his control. The best of collections are always incomplete; for that is the charm and joy of all collecting. Such a collection as this is so far from completion that it can serve only as a hint of what might, with time and energy and camera-enthusiasm, be done. It has been grouped roughly in a sequence of seasons, Shetland seasons, fraught with the vagaries of the open ocean; and in merging and over-lapping have, I am sure, produced varying conflicts of their own. So their chronological order must not be taken too literally. Nor is any single photograph claimed to be wholly representative in itself. The picture which I have endeavoured to produce is not to be found, if it is to be found at all, on any single page, but rather in the impression which the sequence and pattern of the photographs as a whole may succeed in producing.

A wave breaks. The camera registers a visual record of a split second of its thundering onslaught. But it is the unending successive impact of sea upon land which pounds out the stern background against which island-life exists. Literature records fleeting aspects only; a handful of snap-shots the most superficial of fleeting glimpses. Comprehensive vision finds consummation only in the human mind, piecing frail fragments together. Here, then, are a few pages from a photographer's notebook, and, with them, the reader must piece together his own picture as best he can.

Small sea cave: Gruting Voe

SUMMER

THESE pages are opened upon summer. It might have seemed more logical, more in keeping with a conception of beginning and end, to have begun in spring and ended in winter. To have written *finis* at a season associated with fulfilment and finality, in the bleak days which call for nothing more than a solemn requiem, a final benediction. The subject is Shetland: it calls for no such treatment.

So we begin in summer, and *finis* will be written when spring is in full awakening; and the word shall convey its simplest import—the end of a snap-shotter's notes: nothing more.

Summer—with its long days, its periods of great beauty in surroundings most pleasant; its longer periods of cold and wet in surroundings grey and forbidding under bleak and leaden skies. We are apt to remember the rare moments and to forget the unrelenting spells of cold and wet. They go hand in hand. And if the pleasant hours intensify, by contrast, the discomforts of cold and clammy winds, they in turn give fresh loveliness to hours of quiet and sunshine in a land of little isles.

Shetland—a land of little islands—Looking south from Weisdale

Part of Lerwick Harbour, from the Town Hall, with Bressay across the water, and beyond Bressay, the Noup of Noss

LERWICK

LERWICK, a grey stone-built town, stands with its fore-front in the sea, out of which it has risen. It owes its existence to a combination of circumstances—its place as a herring fishing port, arising out of its natural harbour facilities, and also as an island point of entry and exit, now also shared by Sumburgh airfield.

It is the main administrative, social and trading centre of the Islands, but has no substantial hinterland, either agricultural or industrial. Its population is about five thousand.

Lerwick, from the Staney Hill, with the square tower of the Town Hall to the left, and the Wart of Bressay in the distance

South End: Lerwick

Sunlit water near St. Ninian's Isle

THE SEA

SHETLAND cannot be disassociated from the sea. The sea is its dominant element. It is surrounded and cut into by the sea until its most inland sanctuary is no more than three miles from tidal water. At times its whole atmosphere is so saturated by driving sea vapour that no blade of grass escapes the salt tang of the surrounding ocean.

Shetlanders, in general, turn to the sea casually; and going to sea is not for them a wildly adventuresome undertaking, but the more customary way of earning a living. At one time there existed a class of crofter-fishermen whose subsistence came mainly from line-fishing in open boats for ling and cod comparatively near the land, with subsidiary fishings for cod from larger vessels on the Shetland deep-sea fishing grounds, and from smacks and schooners on the cod-banks of Faroe, Rockall and Iceland. The rise of the better compensated and less strenuous herring fishery in the early eighties of the last century, crowned with the advent of the steam trawler, put an end to a mode of livelihood which, as experienced by the fishermen themselves, was a saga of skill, toil, hazard and scanty reward.

It is a natural transition from fishing to sea-going in the merchant service, and to-day the majority of young men are sea-men. Most of them retain homes in the Islands, and their coming and going, linking as it does their firesides with the great ports of the world, has undoubtedly had a profound influence on the whole character of the Shetland people.

Breakers, near Lerwick

Gannets (*Sula bassana*, Brisson)

SEA-BIRDS

Sᴇᴀ-ʙɪʀᴅs in quantity are Shetland's contribution to the bird-life of Britain. The number of Britain's nesting species diminish as one goes northward, but there are certain birds which nest only in the north and of these Shetland has a few—the Great Skua, the Arctic Skua, the Red-throated Diver, and another, the Fulmar Petrel, which first nested in Shetland about seventy years ago, and has now carried its vigorous colonisation southward along the coasts of Scotland to England, Wales and Ireland.

Common Guillemots (*Uria aalge aalge*, Pontoppidan) and Kittiwakes (*Larus tridactylus*, Linnaeus)

Great Skua (*Stercorarius skua skua*, Brunnich)

Red-throated Diver (*Colymbus stellatus*, Pontoppidan)

Fulmar Petrel (*Fulmarus glacialis*, Linnaeus)

Arctic Skua (*Stercorarius parasiticus*, Linnaeus)

Sea Campions (*Silene maritima*, Sm.)

FLOWERS

SUMMER travels north slowly; and the retarding hand which latitude lays upon island plant-life seems only to increase the urgency with which it bursts into bloom once that hand is raised. Those parts of the landscape which in winter were running streams and flooded quagmires become, suddenly, a pattern of gold by the almost riotous blooming of Marsh Marigolds.

All plant-life in Shetland suffers from the constant cropping of the open hillsides by the island sheep; probably the introduction of sheep denuded the islands of trees. A few dwarfed specimens may still be found in inaccessible places, and deep in the peat decayed roots and branches bear evidence of the trees which once existed.

But where there is protection, in enclosed places and on isolated spots, small islands, and on the cliff-face, summer still flaunts a profusion of wild flowers.

Thrift (*Armeria maritima*, Willd.)

Several of the small fresh-water lochs are dotted white with water lilies.

WATER LILIES, peculiar to a few lochs in Shetland, are not found in Orkney; and, while they may have been a local importation, it is interesting to note that 170 years ago George Low, in his *Tours of Orkney and Schetland in 1774*, wrote, "At some distance is Longa Water, where I found the *Nymphæa alba* or Great White Water Lilly in great plenty, the only time I have seen it in Orkney or Schetland, nor do I think it is to be found any where else thro' them."

Glimpses of a small island from which the scent of thrift and vernal squill intermingled float as from a tropic coast

SHETLAND BOATS

IT is sometimes stated that all Shetlanders are boatmen: this is not the case. There are Shetlanders who know little or nothing of boats, who even hesitate to step into a boat, and many who are too engrossed with other matters to be interested.

But the smooth waters of the voes make boating a natural pastime, and, not so long ago, the lack of roads and land transport made it a necessity—it still is in some places. The sea-faring of the past and present generations of men and youths has made boating an occupation and an art. It is natural, therefore, that an unusually large proportion of the population has an affinity for boats and boating.

This Shetland boat—there is an air of tradition about it reminiscent of its Scandinavian origins. Obviously related to the Norse long-ship, its lines are eloquent of a people's dealings with the North Atlantic over a few centuries. If conforms to essential requirements—seaworthiness, strength, and sufficient lightness to be handled on land. It attained its greatest dimensions in the sixern, about thirty-three feet long, between eight and nine feet broad, three

Man's work: Nature's background

The lug-sail race

feet deep, with a keel twenty-one feet in length. The largest sixern built in Shetland was over thirty-eight feet long, eleven feet broad, four feet deep, with a keel twenty-six feet long. The sixern was the principal Shetland fishing-craft of the first half, and continued to hold a significant place well through the second half, of the last century.

The most usual size of Shetland boat is about seventeen-and-a-half feet long, five-and-a-half feet broad, two feet deep, with a keel length of about eleven feet. This is essentially a utility craft. It may be found in sheltered nooks all round the shores, tucked away with a minimum of protection from the elements, some of the boats new and serviceable, others with grass growing through their rotting bottoms, the bulk of them somewhat neglected, reflecting the newer age of swift-wheeled land traffic, which has lowered many sails and taken many oars out of the water.

They sail well, so well that they have tended to produce racing models of their type, and, if properly handled, can withstand considerable stress of weather. They have few of the comforts now embodied in pleasure craft, but they do provide their share of the joys which all small sail boats have to offer.

Regattas—Standing lug-sail and jib: the start

Assembling for a day's racing

A young Viking

Flit-boat, taking passengers ashore from
the inter-island steamer at Mid Yell

Landing barrels in preparation for the herring fishing

HERRING INDUSTRY

ERRING fishing was first introduced to this country by the Dutch, who, although they cured their catches on board, made Bressay Sound their base for the fishing season. In fact it was mainly in this way that Lerwick first began to assume its importance in the Islands.

As the herring fishing developed in this country Lerwick grew in importance, first, as a place at which the herrings were landed and cured, and, second, as the port from which they were exported direct to the Continent.

Drifters crowding in to have their catches sold by auction

A herring station, where the fish are cured

Young Great Skuas (*Stercorarius skua skua*, Brunnich)

YOUNG BIRDS

THE amusing thing about young birds is that often, the younger they are, the older they look. This applies particularly to owls and hawks. Owls have nested in Shetland but only as a very rare occurrence; and of the hawks, the two falcons, the Peregrine and the Merlin, are the only two regular nesters.

The White-tailed Eagle was still nesting in island cliffs in the early years of the century, and last nested in the Neeps of Graveland, on the west coast of Yell, in 1910. The nest was robbed by an egg-collector and from that year the Sea Eagle ceased to be a British nesting species.

Young Manx Shearwater (*Puffinus puffinus puffinus*)

Young Hooded Crows (*Corvus cornix*, Linnaeus)

Young Common Tern (*Sterna hirundo*, Linnaeus)

Young Shags (*Phalacrocorax graculus*, Linnaeus)

Young Gannets (*Sula bassana*, Brisson)

Young Merlins (*Falco columbarius aesalon*, Tunstall)

Friendly overtures

PONIES

SHETLAND ponies roam the hills pretty much at will; but they are not wild in the sense that rabbits are called wild. Each one is very much somebody's property. And generally their movements are confined to the narrow limits of prescribed grazings. They live almost entirely on these common pastures, and prefer to feed in the damp marshy places.

In the summer they shed their winter coats and, for a time, become extremely tattered and unkempt; but once this stage is over they look their part— the vigorous tough breed which the rigours of centuries have produced.

Shetland ponies

Shedding his coat

MIDSUMMER EVENING

ONE aspect of summer is emphasised in Shetland—the long hours of daylight. The summer day lengthens until at midsummer darkness exists only for an hour or two. Shetland is no land of the midnight sun; one must travel four hundred miles farther north for that. And for twenty-four hours of continuous sunshine, sacrifice the one thing which makes the sun's course a grand pageant, its daily disappearance from view. Its sunset and sunrise.

The peculiar quality of those long summer days which seem to fascinate so many people who experience them in their kindlier moods, and which remain an abiding memory to Shetlanders who have gone abroad, lies not in the hours of full light but in the hours of dusk.

The long periods of half-light soften the sharp outlines and tone down the clear contrasts of daytime. They transform harsh contours, ugly shapes, jarring colours, and link up broken aspects in gracious continuity. An atmosphere of unreality grows, a sense of mystery envelopes, a veil of make-believe settles over everything.

Dim hills reflected in the calm waters of narrow voes, birds calling over the sea, a dog barking at its own echoing voice, dark reflections of small boats at anchor—in such expressions of a twilit eve does Shetland claim an aspect of summer peculiarly her own.

Eider duck on nest

A midsummer, midnight photograph: Lerwick Harbour, 12 midnight, June

Land and sea, interlocked: Whiteness

AUTUMN

AUTUMN is no certain period of mellow sunshine. Wind and rain may, in an afternoon, damage severely a summer's crop. The sky may be overcast for days on end. But of all the seasons, it has, perhaps, the most to offer. Temperatures are beginning to fall, but there is a summer's warmth in soil and sea; darkness may be returning, but its footfall is, at first, almost imperceptible. "The nights are beginning to creep in," folks say.

40

Young Fulmars, greyish white blobs against their darker background, slowly developing from oversized powder-puffs towards full-fledging and departure, still occupy secure niches in the cliffs. Under boulders and in the ruins of old walls, Storm Petrels still come fluttering at midnight to feed chicks in feathery down; and in the sky, thousands of other birds, swinging high against white battlements of cloud, wheel in restless masses, a mounting presage of impending migration.

The green cornfields begin to pale.

Young Fulmar (*Fulmarus glacialis*, Linnaeus)

A catch of sea-trout

TROUT FISHING

SALMON are not native to Shetland waters; and the smallness of the streams, generally, makes the successful introduction of salmon highly problematic. The combination of burns, voes, and extensive shingly fore-shores has given the Islands a reputation for Sea Trout, but the numbers of fish have fallen off during the past twenty years.

Trout population is determined to a considerable extent by factors which could be brought under human control; and Shetland has here a rich field for scientific investigation and enlightened development. So far, this field has been touched only by anglers; and angling, a combination of fishing rights and rites of *diptera* worship no less sacred, provides, as all good anglers know, the very minimum, if not the complete negation, of mental effort of any kind.

The remains of a prehistoric trap for catching trout: Known as a *laxigert*

Fishing trout in the open sea

HERRING FISHING ENDS

EARLY autumn sees the end of the herring fishing. Drifters and motor-boats go south to continue operations from the East Coast of England. Hundreds of fish-workers, women and men, who had come north when the fishing commenced, shut up their temporary summer homes and follow the fishing fleet. From the quays thousands of barrels of salted herrings are taken by flit-boats to be loaded into steamers lying in the fairway of Lerwick Harbour.

Like a recurring stampede this mobile industry crowds in upon Lerwick almost overnight each year, and fades away almost as suddenly; and its whole content and character, its scramble and gamble, is not far removed from the uncertainty of the gold rushes of half-a-century ago. At least, such were the conditions in pre-war days.

Herring gulls crowd the quays at Lerwick

Herring ready for shipment to the Continent—in the centre a flit-boat, by means of which the barrels are conveyed to the steamers loading in the fairway

Motorboats

Evening sunshine on Scalloway

THE WEST-SIDE

Aɴ island group stretching in a north and south direction naturally becomes divided into east and west sides. The Mainland of Shetland, moreover, bulges out to the west and this substantial area also comes under the term, West-side.

Having hills behind to give shelter from the cold east winds, and facing the setting sun, is an aspect which means much in the north; and this perhaps

The cliffs on the west meet the full impact of the Atlantic

Looking west from the Scord of Scalloway

gives the west something, especially in the matter of growing things, which

the east has not. Certainly, in an autumn evening, Scalloway, almost floodlit

by the setting sun, presents an atmosphere of sunny warmth with which the

grey, eastward-looking Lerwick cannot compete.

And, looking out to the west, away to the horizon, the high, clean-cut, hilltops of Foula, in their varying shades of blue and purple, add to the view that sense of distance which helps to link the sunset itself with the land and sea, and so, inwards, to the near and immediate surroundings.

A West-side view, with Foula in the distance

A young Grey Seal

SEALS

SEALS are shot for their skins, but not to the extent of threatening their existence as a common mammal. The Grey Seal is protected.

On the remoter islands both species may be seen in fairly large numbers; and young Common Seals, attracted by shoals of fish to the quaysides of Lerwick Harbour, may often be watched at close quarters.

Young Grey Seals, which in the early weeks of their lives live on land, may be found on a few of the more difficult and remote parts of the coast, but as these young seals are born in the late autumn, weather conditions usually make approach more or less hazardous.

With seals, one associates porpoises, dolphins and whales; these can all be seen on occasion, and on one very unique occasion, a few years ago, a walrus visited the Shetland coast for some weeks, and was actually photographed in the vicinity of Lerwick.

Seals basking

Leading home the winter's fuel

PONIES AT WORK

SHETLAND ponies are used for drawing small carts and, occasionally, for light ploughing, but in the past their main use has been to convey peats over hillsides void of any cart-tracks.

Modern road-making, and the use of motor lorries in conveying peats from greater distances, has reduced this use of ponies, but the practice still exists in some localities, and provides one of the happiest examples of man-cum-animal activity in the whole calendar of crofting life.

The foal stands by while the mother is being loaded up

Ponies and foals move nimbly over the rough ground

CROFTS

However small a croft may be, it stands a monument to man's struggle with nature, a tribute to hard toil, to courage and ingenuity. To-day, it is a monument to a struggle continuing or to a struggle ended.

The croft has ceased to be in itself an adequate means of livelihood, and tends more and more to become an adjunct to some form of wage-earning.

The future of Shetland crofting is the Islands' biggest problem.

Crofts: Fogrigarth

Croft: Foula

All that remains of a croft—one of hundreds of homesteads abandoned

CONTACTS

SHETLAND's links with the world through her seamen and through those who have gone abroad and made their homes in other countries have also a complementary link with the Continent of Europe through the herring industry.

At one time, Lerwick was a centre for the Dutch herring fishing, but with the evolution of larger fishing craft and the introduction of motor propulsion the necessity for entering port so often was reduced, and the number of Dutch vessels visiting Lerwick Harbour steadily decreased until, in the 1930's, the final collapse of the Dutch herring fishing brought an end to an association picturesque no less than cordial. The echoing of wooden clogs

A mixed collection of British and foreign fishing craft in Lerwick Harbour

The barque, SVERRE, of Finland, the last square-rigged vessel to discharge cargo at Lerwick; probably the last of its kind ever to visit the Islands

Dutch fishermen

Swedish line-fishers

on Lerwick's narrow, stone-paved streets and lanes will always remain a pleasant memory for those old enough to recall the annual coming of the Hollanders.

Norwegian and Swedish fishing boats still call, but mainly to buy fresh mackerel from the British drifters for curing, and also for bait for line fishing. Very recent visits from Norwegian whale-catchers are reminiscent of a period in the first quarter of the century during which Norwegian whaling companies operated from voes in the north of the Shetland mainland.

The main market for herring has always been a Continental market, but the representatives of Germany, Poland, the Baltic countries and Russia have not been foreign fishermen, but foreign merchants, or, more often, their own or their British representatives.

ATMOSPHERE

THE import of autumn is something very real in experience, yet, for the photographer, almost out of reach.

Colour, temperature, the feel of gathering strength in a passing gust of wind, a deeper note in the surge of the sea, the winter call of a bird, all manifestations which combine to create a quality, an atmosphere, which keeps just beyond his grasp. Where there are fallen leaves and thinning branches he seizes upon them, but on the bare hills of a rocky island there are few aids, and he faces one of the challenges which has still to be mastered.

Rugged and sunlit—an uninviting bit of coast

Britain's farthest north lighthouse station—the Shore Station, Muckle Flugga

A BUILDING suddenly bright against its background of brown hill; a gable-
end shining like a star in the dusk; such afternoon gleams of light are
but reminders that the autumn sun is already low in the sky.

Autumn evening sunlight

A last use for a Shetland boat—as a roof to shelter sheep in winter

WINTER

WIND, rain, and long hours of darkness, these are the more usual concomitants of a Shetland winter. But, like the other seasons, winters, too, vary considerably. Some are almost without snow, others are a sequence of snow and sleet, of freezing and thawing.

On rare occasions there may be intervals of comparatively mild weather; or a spell of still, calm, frosty quiet, with the white hills reflected in the dark voes—where the water has not become dulled by a thin coating of ice.

Bright moonlight, or even bright starlight alone, may give these nights a

A pony that can fend for itself in all weathers

Snow

sparkling brilliance. And there are nights when the Merry Dancers, *Aurora borealis*, throw a waltzing luminescence over the land and water.

But in the main it is a period for indoor life, for indoor amusements, and for sheltering from the elements.

Wind

WIND AND SEA

Two intermediaries for photographing the wind that blows are sea-gulls
on the wing, and the week's washing on the clothesline; the clothes,
imprisoned, and fighting to be free; the gulls, free, and riding this unruly
element with apparent zest.

The sea needs no intermediary: its visible splendour mounts with its might,
and its winter blows are the embodiment of sheer physical power and fury.

Sea

Storm

COMMUNICATIONS

COMMUNICATIONS between the Islands are limited, and, in some cases, inadequate. The mail-boat which crosses more than a dozen miles of the open Atlantic from Foula to the mainland of Shetland is a small open motorboat of less than five tons gross. Each time it returns to Foula it has to be taken to a place of safety over a rough beach, mainly by man-handling. This necessity precludes a larger boat being used.

The mails to and from Papa Stour are taken across Papa Sound, a notorious piece of tidal water, in an open sailboat.

Telephone communication by radio beam has helped to eliminate total isolation of the more remote islands, but there is a need of greater facilities if these communities are to survive. Air transport, if it comes soon enough, may solve some of the problems.

Launching the Foula mail-boat

The Atlantic swell

Linking the Islands together by beam telephone

SHIPS

LYING on a North Atlantic sea route, Shetland's association with ships, and especially with ships in sail, is a story mostly of tragic happenings. Ships have found refuge, lives have been saved, but the tale is one mainly of disaster.

Any detailed record of those shipwrecks would provide a rough indication of European economic development over centuries; and would at times touch closely not only some of the greater moments in European history, but also various phases of world crisis and achievement.

Like a second doorway, the cavity under the floor houses the horizontal mill-wheel, called the *tirl*

SHETLAND WATERMILL

ABOUT the beginning of the century every croft had its watermill or, where the mill was owned by a group of crofts, its share in a watermill, as was often the case. It was an essential part of the croft functioning as a self-contained economic unit.

A noted archaeologist wrote, 'This type of mill is actually mentioned in ninth-century papers, and is one of the oldest in existence. In a few years it will be a thing of the past, yet it remains one of the most remarkable examples of hydromechanics'. Already, it may be called a 'thing of the past'. There is scarcely a burn in the Islands which does not have the remains of one or several of those mills.

Watermill driven by water diverted from a burn

The *tirl*, which is attached by a shaft direct to the upper millstone is turned by the water directed by a sluice on blades to one side of the vertical shaft

A portion of the prehistoric buildings excavated from the sand at Jarlshof, Sumburgh

PREHISTORIC REMAINS

PREHISTORIC remains are likely to be more numerous in localities where the material used was of necessity durable; and in these Islands, where wood was no doubt scarce and stone plentiful, ancient buildings of many kinds are common. A few have been excavated by competent archaeologists, but the majority have been burrowed into casually by the curious, and very many have been removed in part or altogether by those who saw only convenient sources of building material for their immediate needs.

Four of the few
stone arrow-
heads found in
Shetland
(in the hand)

Stone relics of
prehistoric times

Another corner
of the Jarlshof
excavations

Snow, and winter sunshine

SNOW

No Shetland winter passes without a fall of snow at some time or other, but winters with prolonged periods of snow are the exception. Occasionally the Islands experience a spell of snowy conditions that is crisp and cold and dry, but this is unusual. Alternating frost and rain, hail and sleet, combined with the thawing action of the salt-laden atmosphere on fallen snow, make snowy weather, generally, unpleasant more often than not.

Croft, under snow

Lerwick, from Upper Sound

Intervals of winter quiet: At sunrise

At sunset

UP-HELLY-AA

NEAR the end of January, each year in peace times, Lerwick organises a torch-light procession, called Up-Helly-Aa, culminating in the burning of a dramatised model of a Norse war-galley. The conception is no doubt derived from an earlier practice of burning a tar-barrel, a custom familiar to other parts of Scotland. This modern version, however, if somewhat obscure in its historical origins, does not lack for youthful exuberance and enthusiasm, and comes as a diversion at a time of year when entertainment has its greatest value.

Bow of an Up-Helly-Aa galley, with Guizer Jarl and some of his crew

SPRING

SPRING comes late in Shetland, but it comes with a bound, hurrying to make up for lost time. When it is later than usual, it arrives with almost Arctic precipitancy, and flowers leap out of the barren, wind-swept, spray-bleached countryside.

And even so, Winter may steal back for a parting reminder, pelting astonished lambs with hailstones and covering young crops with snow.

April and early May are Shetland's springtime, period of bright sunshine and snowy clouds, and, as often as not, of north-east winds that cut to the bone.

Marsh marigolds (*Caltha palustris*, Linnaeus)

Hooded Crow (*Corvus cornix*, Linnaeus)

The shepherd

TOP RIGHT - Primroses (*Primula vulgaris*, Linnaeus)

CONTRASTS

ONE of the most severe snow blizzards ever experienced in Shetland occurred with great suddenness on April 27, 1927. Yet there have been years when April was a better month than any month of the summer that followed.

It is a season with a fine range of surprising contrasts, not to mention the range of its contrasting surprises. A great month for the photographer—visibility, cloud, atmosphere, in a constant state of change, rich with the possibilities that may, without warning, suddenly combine to present the opportunity for a masterpiece.

One of the knitting needles is lodged in a padded belt worn for the purpose

HAND-KNITTING

KNITTING is Shetland's most extensive and most firmly established industry. Not only have the capable hands of Shetland women been employed knitting a varity of articles for centuries, but it might also be said that they have, on occasion, been engaged in knitting together the very economic texture of the community. Fishings have failed, crops have failed, trade stagnation has discharged hundreds of men from sea-going employment; always, as a last insurance against calamity, there has been the women's knitting.

82

It is neither a highly remunerative nor a particularly healthy occupation, rather the reverse. It has grown up as part of a crofting economy, and tends to survive lean times which would normally spell ruin to a more complex method of production.

War years, which diverted large scale machine production in the woollen industries to other work, have given knitters their most prosperous periods. But between the wars, when hand-made articles had to compete with factory-made goods, the knitters' returns in terms of labour and time were meagre indeed.

Recent years have shown a great advance in the quality of the goods, particularly in respect of colour, pattern and design.

Boat repairs on the seashore

THE VOAR

To a Shetlander the word *voar* means not only springtime but also the crofting activities with which it is associated. In some respects it is the most back-breaking season of the year. Manuring, digging, sowing and planting; cutting peats; the lambing, and a score of other jobs for which the lengthening days are never long enough.

A ploughman's team

Peat casting

The catch

A study in curves

A typical group of Puffins (*Fratercula arctica*, Linnaeus)

PUFFINS

IN SUMMER and early autumn there are immense congregations of puffins on the Isle of Foula, and at Hermaness, in Unst; at dozens of other places round the coast, where nesting conditions are suitable, smaller colonies exist, some of a few pairs, others of a few thousands. The puffin is interested in land only during the nesting season: at other times it cleaves to the open ocean and eschews all land like the plague.

Puffins have to be seen to be believed; their small rotund figures, snow-white fronts, bright yellow legs, outrageously rouged aristocratic beaks, their

A common posture

A Photograph which shows the beautiful wing of the Puffin

small neat wings fold with previse over-lapping tips.

Their mannerisms are the embodiment of the serio-comic; posturing as if immersed in profound thought; gravely immobile, suddenly to break out into agitated movement as if forgotten engagements had suddenly come to mind.

They have powerful enemies, among them the Great Skua and the Great Black-backed Gull, but they rely very successfully on their agility in the air to outwit and out-manœuvre these marauders.

The young, a single bird in each nest, are reared in burrows and crevices underground; they are fed on beakfuls of sand-eel and herring-fry brought in from the open sea.

Sheep dog

Four-horned ram

ANIMALS

IN a crofting, as distinct from the larger farming, community, animals may receive such close and personal attention as to become familiar personalities in themselves, calling for consideration quite outside the requirements of economic husbandry. A hen, living to be a score of years old; a cow, dying of old age; these incidents occur. And if they do not conform to the requirements of successful modern farming, they do show that intimate contact between animals and man without which modern farming could not have developed.

A sheep carrying a device which deters it from pushing through wire fences to raid enclosed crops

AT the same time, we find that the testing of cattle for bovine tubercu-losis has shown Shetland cattle to be practically 100 per cent free from this disease; and with the complete attestation, at an early date, of all herds in the Islands, Shetland will take its place as the first county in Britain to attain complete certified immunity.

A Shetland foal

YOUTH

To a world emerging from its second world war, and endeavouring to regain some measure of new hope and encouragement for the future, new emphasis is being laid upon the needs of Youth. More facilities, better opportunities for youthful activities are being demanded; we are living in a period of incipient Youth Movements.

If there is a picture which, more than any other, epitomises the spirit of island youth at its best, it is perhaps that of an island boat, under sail, with Youth at the helm.

FINIS

AND

A SMALL TAILPIECE

Shetland Wren (*Troglodytes troglodytes zetlandicus*)

And why
shouldn't I
be in!

Lund Humphries 6.48.19040

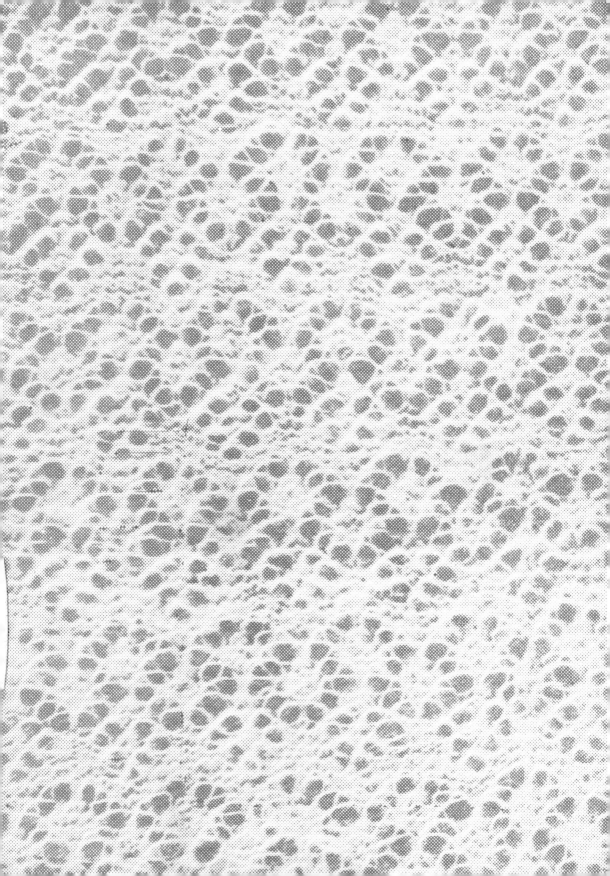